Contents

Introduction 3

What is the 2 Position System? 4

Octaves and the Warp Factor 7
   The Warp Factor 7

Okay, I understand the theory but how do I practice this? 10

Deeper into the Warp Zone 11

Scale Pairs 14

Stacking the Patterns 18
   Combining Patterns 18

Open Position Scales with the 2 Position System 20

Arpeggios and the 2 Position System 22
   3-Note Arpeggios 22
      Major Arpeggios 24
      Diminished Arpeggios 25
      Augmented Arpeggios 26
   4-Note Arpeggios 26
      Major 7 Arpeggio (1, 3, 5, 7) 27
      Minor 7 Arpeggio (1, b3, 5, b7) 27
      Dominant 7 Arpeggio (1, 3, 5, b7) 28
      Minor 7b5 Arpeggio (1, b3, b5, b7) 28
      Minor Major 7 Arpeggio (1, b3, 5, 7) 28
   How to Go Beyond 4-Note Arpeggios 29
   The 2 Position System Applied to Extended Arpeggios 29
      Major 7 Arpeggio Extensions 30
   General Rules for Arpeggio Construction 32

Useful Scales Section 34
   Minor Scales 34

Major Scales *37*
Dominant 7 Scales *39*
Other Useful Scales *40*

More from Unlock the Guitar **42**

Introduction

This book builds on the **2 Position Scale System Introductory Book** by expanding the reach of the 2 Position System to include how to change between scales, open position scales, how to stack the positions to form larger ones, and a new section which incorporates arpeggios into the system.

The premise of this system has always been to focus on the musical aspect of scales, and now arpeggios, instead of the endless memorization of patterns and permutations you get with other systems such the CAGED and 3NPS ones, which means there's far too much time wasted before they become useful. Don't get me wrong, this is not a book of shortcuts. You'll still have to put the work in to get good results, but know that we've reduced that amount of 'work', or 'woodshedding' by about 80%.

What you'll get from this system is a profound insight into how the guitar, in standard tuning, can be understood to effortlessly learn the tools for confident improvisation: scales and arpeggios.

To your best playing yet,

Graham

www.unlocktheguitar.net

What is the 2 Position System?

The basic premises of the 2 Position System are:

-Small useable chunks of information which can be easily learned/internalized.

-Easy to move the information around/change keys.

-Streamlined thinking to concentrate on the music rather than learning endless permutations of scale patterns.

-Make practicing scales more productive, musical and fun.

-Learn any scale across the whole fretboard in a matter of hours not weeks, months or years.

In the 2 Position System, we can cover the entire fretboard, including open positions, using only two scale patterns. I call them the **forward position** and the **backward position**, though you can name them how you wish as this is merely to identify them.

The forward position goes up the neck in one octave. Let's use A natural minor (A Aeolian) starting on the low E string as an example.

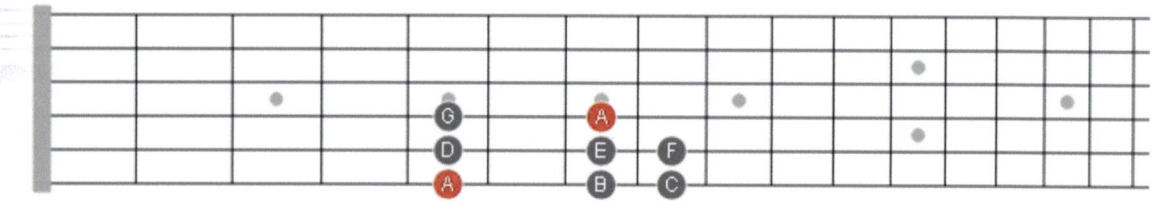

This shouldn't take you long to learn at all if you aren't already familiar with it. Once you've got the pattern down **STOP** playing it as a scale. The only function of playing a scale in note order up and down is to get it from this page into your memory. Once you know it, don't play it as a scale. We want to avoid the pitfall of running up and down scales as whatever you practice will inevitably show up in your playing.

The next task is to improvise with this scale fragment. Get someone to play an Am or Am7 chord for you, or even an A drone will do. See how much mileage you can get out if this pattern—you'll be surprised. **PRACTICING A SCALE** means practicing things you might actually play. This is your opportunity to really get to know the sounds of the scale as you're only dealing with one octave at a time. Listen to each note as you play it and be aware of how it sounds against the root.

IMPORTANT: Once you can *see* the pattern clearly on the fretboard, come at it with different fingerings, use fragments of it. In other words, don't stray outside the pattern but do mix up your fingering as much as you can. <u>This is precisely to avoid getting stuck in a rut.</u>

The backward position goes down the neck in the opposite direction. It <u>always</u> shares the same root note as the forward position. Do the same as before, run the scale until you have it down cold then **STOP**. Again, play around with it, make music with it and see what you can come up with.

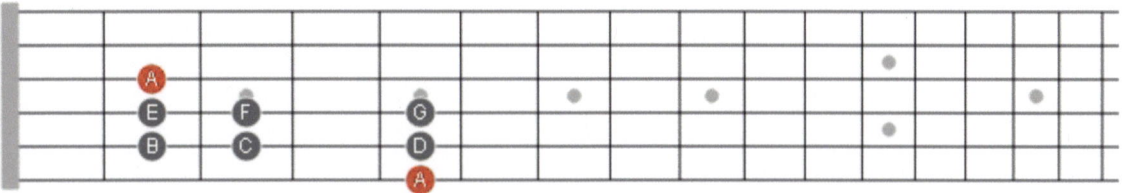

That's it! These are all the patterns we need to play A natural minor anywhere on the fretboard in any key. In the next chapter, we'll look at how to link them.

Octaves and the Warp Factor

Knowing where the octaves are found is critical to be able to connect these two patterns and use the entire fretboard to improvise. Here are the octaves in A:

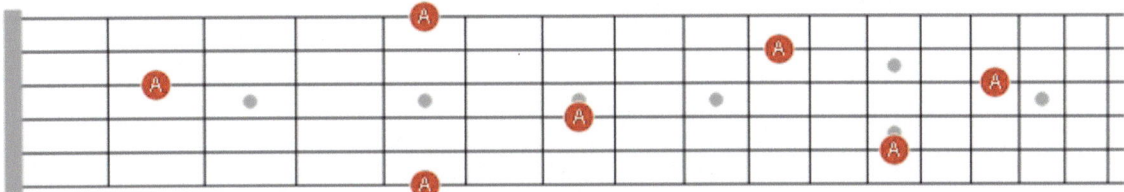

Now, the forward and backward patterns remain the same on the E, A, D, G string set but if we include the B string, things start to get a little warped.

The Warp Factor

Note: If you tune in fourths (E, A, D, G, C, F) then this section does not apply to you. This system really lends itself to the fantastic symmetrical nature of fourths tuning.

The guitar, in standard tuning, is tuned in fourths up until the B string which is a major third from the G string. This causes everything to warp one fret **up** the neck when passing into the B string warp zone but the patterns are essentially the same. It's very important to treat any pattern involving the B string as the same pattern, not a new one. You only want to learn two patterns per scale then get used to warping them up one fret if the B string is involved.

Here's the **forward pattern** on the D, G, B string set. Notice how the B string pushes the G and A notes up one fret but it is still the same pattern. Compare it to the forward pattern below.

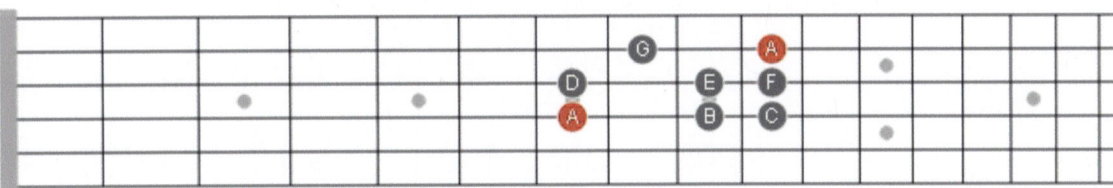

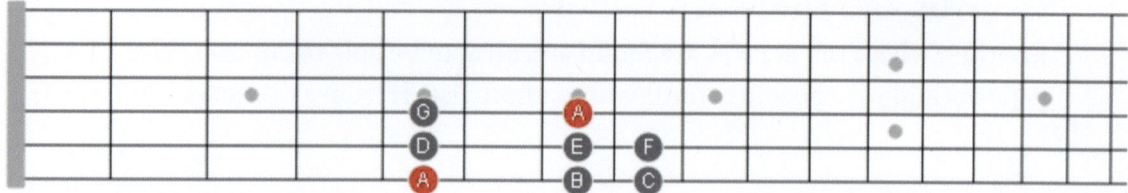

And on the G, B, E string set:

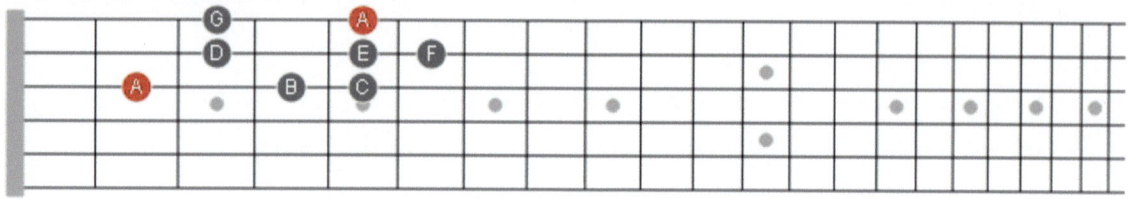

Again, the pattern is the same only warped by the B string. Compare it to the pattern below. Notice how everything is moved up one fret on the B string with the notes on the top E string following suit.

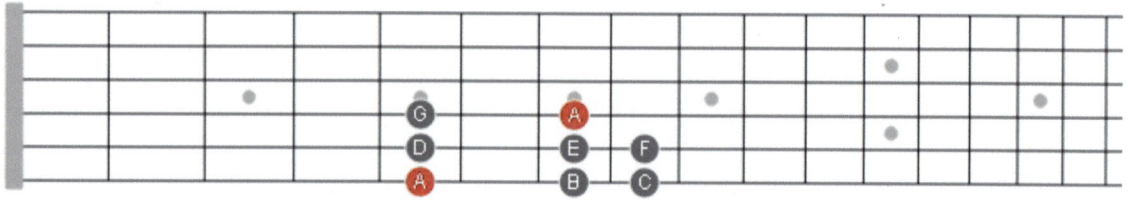

Here's the **backward pattern** on the A, D, G, B string set. Notice how the B string pushes the final A note up one fret but it is still the same pattern.

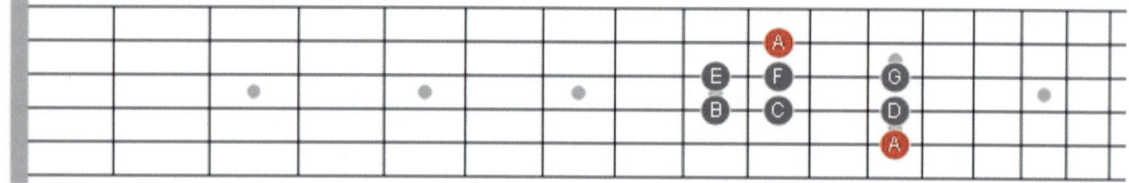

Here's the **backward pattern** on the D, G, B, E string set. Again, notice how the B string pushes everything up one fret with the E string following suit, but it is still the same pattern.

What you're seeing here is simply the same information distorted by the fretboard, almost like an optical illusion. When this information clicks, you're ready for the next chapter!

Okay, I understand the theory but how do I practice this?

Let's go through the steps to learn a scale across the entire fretboard.

Step 1 – Choose a scale you want to learn from the **Scale Reference Section**.

Step 2 – Learn the forward pattern for the scale starting on the root note on the low E string.

Step 3 – Close this book! Don't look at or play the scale pattern in order once you've got them in your head.

Step 4 – Make music with the pattern, play over a drone or a chord, get used to how the scale sounds and have some fun with it. Visualize the pattern but free up your fingers to play fragments of the scale.

Step 5 – Repeat the first four steps for the backward pattern.

Step 6 – Once you feel comfortable venture out of the pattern and into the next octave and start moving around the fretboard. **The important thing here is not to get lost**. If you feel lost go back, there's no rush. This part is a little like learning to speak another language. At first you make small utterances while building your fluency. Don't despair; it doesn't take long to become fluent at this. Make sure you know where you are in the scale at all times, no matter how slowly you have to play.

Step 7 – Practice playing any scale pattern that incorporates either the B string, or the B and E strings. **It's very important that you do this as a mental exercise and not from a diagram**. I have purposely not included any warp diagrams in the Useful Scales Section for this very reason. **This shift must take place in your head**. Once you've been through this process with a few scales it soon becomes second nature.

Congratulations! You've just learned to play a scale over the entire fretboard in the time it takes to learn one position from the 3NPS or CAGED systems!

Deeper into the Warp Zone

The warp zone itself is also a useful area of the fretboard for practicing with scale fragments so for this next section we'll only be using the top two strings (B and E). Once you're within the confines of the warp zone there are no shifts to be made. We'll use the horizontal length of the fretboard to complete the scale.

Again, the idea here is to first get the pattern off the page and into your head. Once it's there close this page. If you make a mistake or get a little lost when moving horizontally, your ears should tell you and you can adjust accordingly.

Here is a selection of scale patterns to start you off practicing this way. Once you get the hang of this you can apply it to any scale pattern in this book. Simply take the notes on the top two strings of the forward pattern and start them on the B string root note. Complete the scale by moving horizontally up and add in the approach note (G in this case) before the root. As you can see these patterns lend themselves well to string bending, single string runs and double stops.

Aeolian Pattern

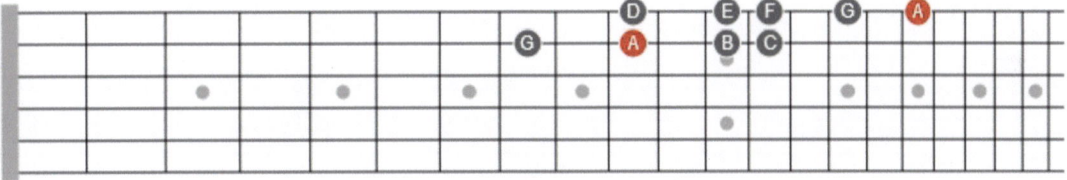

Dorian Pattern

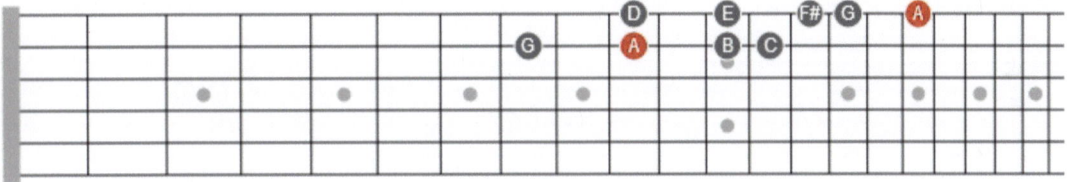

Minor Pentatonic Pattern

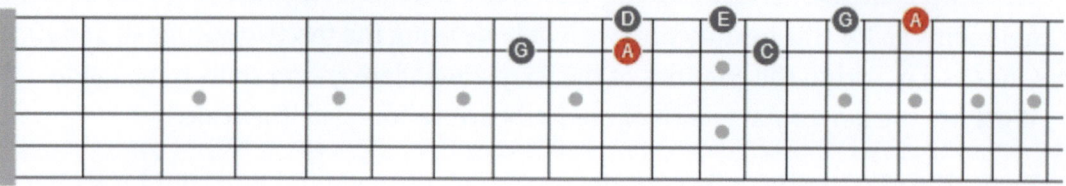

Phrygian Pattern

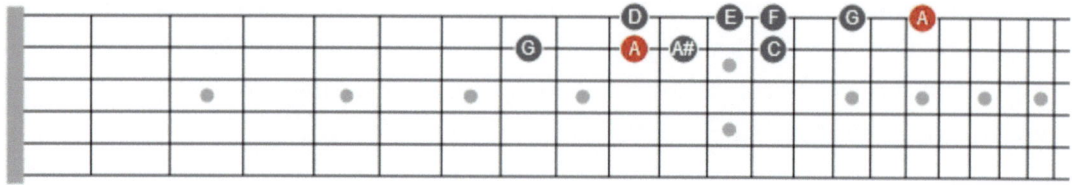

Lydian Pattern

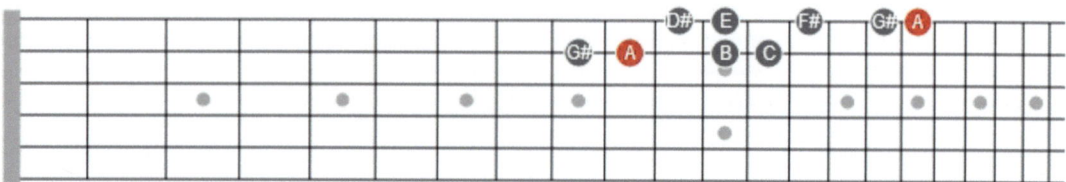

Mixolydian Pattern

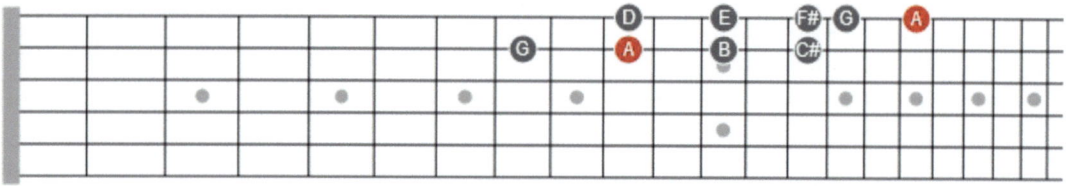

Locrian Pattern

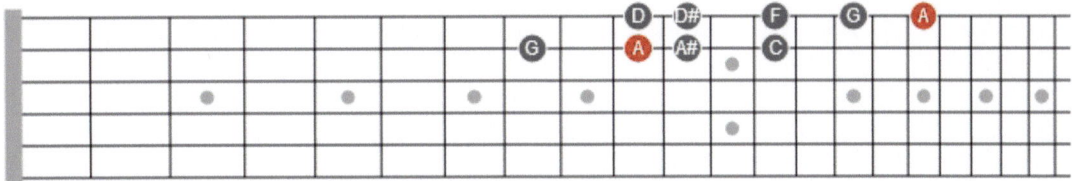

Blues Scale Pattern

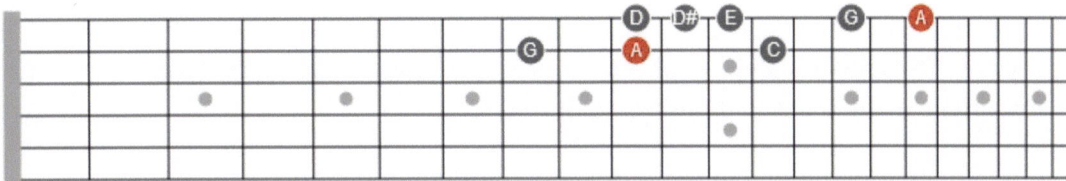

Melodic Minor Pattern

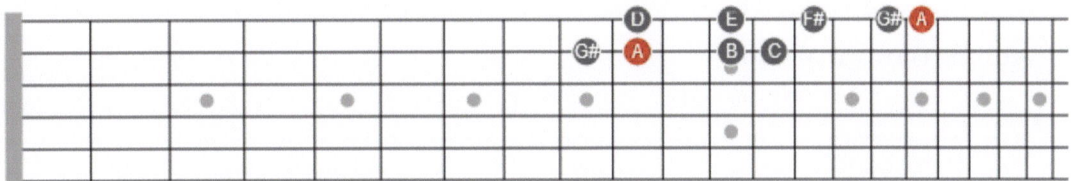

Harmonic Minor Pattern

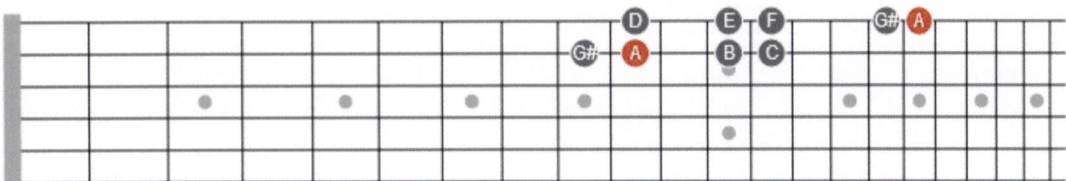

Scale Pairs

Scale Pairs are pairs of scales that differ by one note. For example, if we spell the Natural Minor Scale/Aeolian scale in intervals we get:

1, 2, b3, 4, 5, b6, b7

Then compare it with the Dorian scale:

1, 2, b3, 4, 5, 6, b7

You'll notice that there is only one note which is different, the 6th. Aeolian has a flat 6th while Dorian has a natural 6th.

If you've been learning either of these scales, you'll soon realize that changing one note has a huge impact on the sound of a scale.

One of the advantages of the 2 Position System, as oppose to other systems, is the ease of changing between scales as there's very little to remember. Try doing this with the CAGED or 3NPS systems and you'll see what I mean!

Compare the forward patterns:

Aeolian/Natural Minor

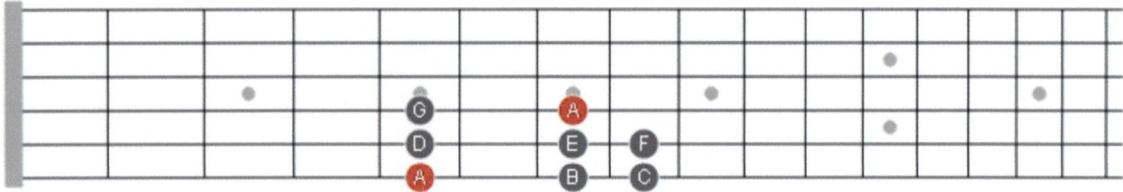

Dorian

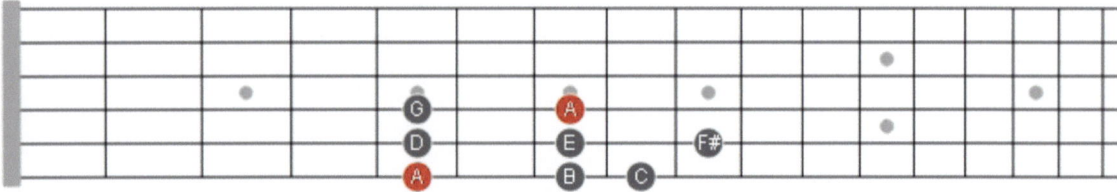

And the backward patterns:

Aeolian/Natural Minor

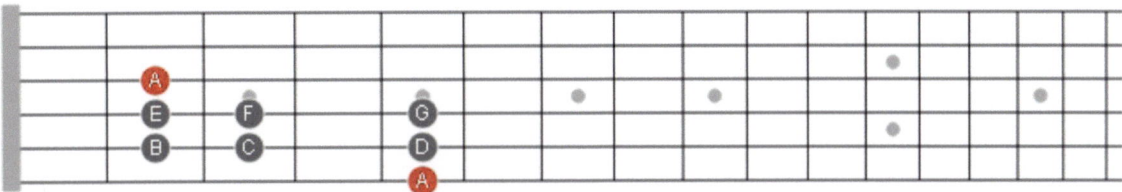

Dorian

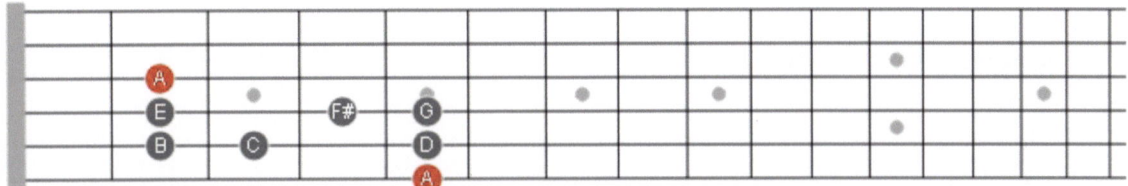

The 6th, in this case F/F#, is the note that changes and with it the sound of the scale. I find the F# lightens the sound somewhat and has a more bluesy vibe.

Since both scales can be used over Am, Am7, Am9, Am11 etc. you now have another option within very easy reach.

How to Practice:

1. Make sure you know the forward and backward patterns for both scales without referring to the diagrams in this book.

2. Practice going back and forth between the scales over a drone or a minor chord. At first it'll sound somewhat forced but play with the concept for a while and you'll soon start to find less obvious ways to change between scales.

3. Once you're comfortable changing between scales start to move around the fretboard. Make sure you don't feel lost, if you do just come back to familiar territory.

Let's look at another example.

Aeolian to Phrygian

Again, there's only a one-note difference between these scales but this time the change in mood is a little more drastic.

Compare the intervals:

Aeolian: 1, 2, b3, 4, 5, b6, b7

Phrygian: 1, b2, b3, 4, 5, b6, b7

The b2 in the Phrygian scale is quite dramatic but when used tastefully it can spice up any solo.

Compare the forward patterns:

Aeolian/Natural Minor

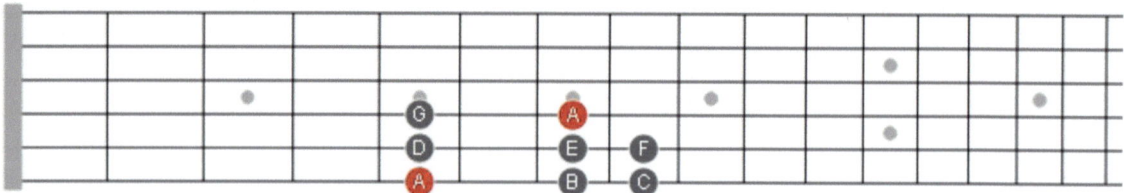

Phrygian

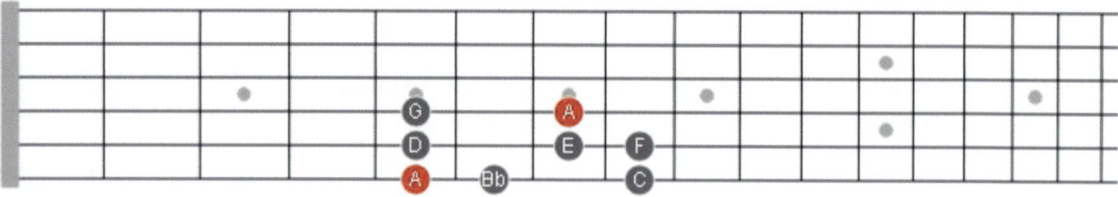

And the backward positions:

Aeolian/Natural Minor

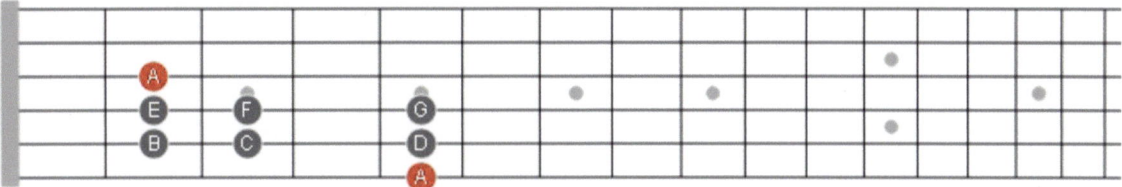

Phrygian

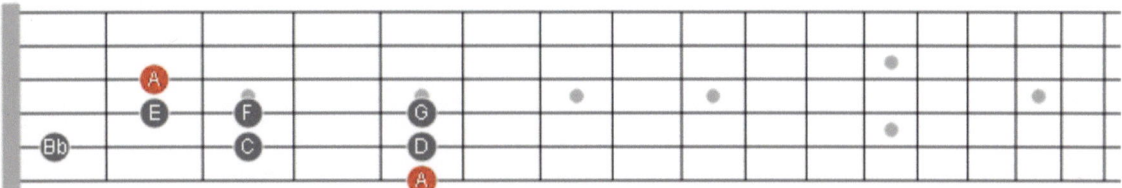

Practice as above. You now have 3 choices for playing over minor or minor 7 chords within easy reach.

Now you've got the idea, practice with the following scale pairs:

Scale Pair	Intervals	Playing Situation
Aeolian/Natural Minor & Harmonic Minor	1, 2, b3, 4, 5, b6, b7 1, 2, b3, 4, 5, b6, 7	Use over minor chords to add exotic tensions
Major Scale & Lydian	1, 2, 3, 4, 5, 6, 7 1, 2, 3, #4, 5, 6, 7	Use over major chords to add that Lydian vibe
Major Scale & Mixolydian	1, 2, 3, 4, 5, 6, 7 1, 2, 3, 4, 5, 6, b7	Use over major chords for a more bluesy feel
Phrygian & Locrian	1, b2, b3, 4, 5, b6, b7 1, b2, b3, 4, b5, b6, b7	Use over minor or m7b5 chords for a darker sound
Melodic Minor & Harmonic Minor	1, 2, b3, 4, 5, 6, 7 1, 2, b3, 4, 5, b6, 7	Use over minor or mM7 chords for an exotic sound
Major Scale & Melodic Minor	1, 2, 3, 4, 5, 6, 7 1, 2, b3, 4, 5, 6, 7	Use for an interesting major to minor sound

There are of course many more combinations of scales which you're sure to pick up on once you start looking for alternative sounds to play over chords.

Stacking the Patterns

As you start to venture out of the first octave and link these patterns vertically and horizontally on the fretboard, you'll notice that they fit together like jigsaw pieces as follows.

Here you can see the forward pattern on the E, A and D strings with the backward pattern stacked on top of it. We'll use the A Aeolian/Natural Minor scale in these examples but you can apply this to any scale, and in any key.

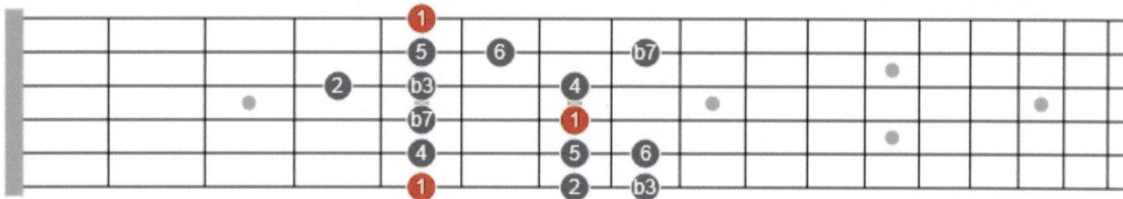

Be sure to keep the 2-pattern methodology in mind, and not revert to learning patterns like these as the temptation will be just to run up and down them. Alternatively, if you're recovering from the CAGED system then you may already know this pattern, only now it's far more usable!

Here's another stacked pattern that fits nicely to the left of the above pattern (if you're playing a righty guitar), and covers frets 2 to 5.

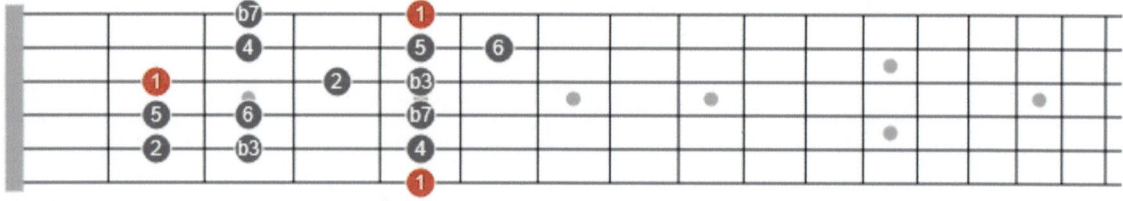

You have the backward pattern on the lower three strings with a warped forward pattern stacked on top. Again, it may look like one of those clunky CAGED patterns, only now you'll be able to navigate it and come up with some lines that don't sound like scales.

Combining Patterns

The patterns with roots on the A string can be combined to great effect with the Scale Fragments we looked at in the last chapter.

Take the following backward pattern:

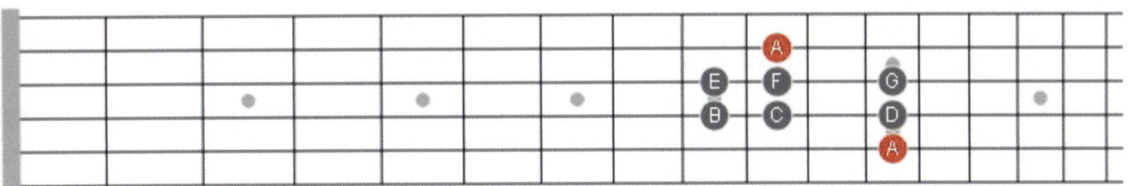

And combine it with the corresponding scale fragment:

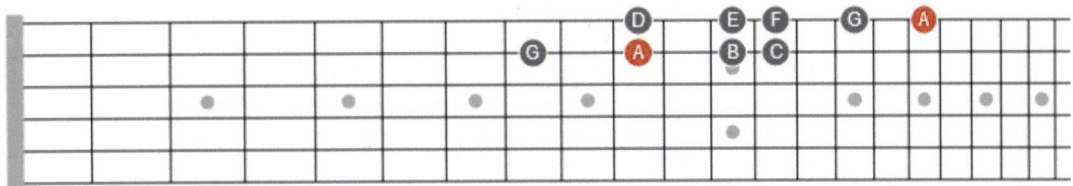

Again, in this example we used the A Aeolian/Natural Minor scale but you can apply this to any scale in this book.

Open Position Scales with the 2 Position System

The 2 Position Scale System also lends itself well to playing in open positions as the same logic applies. To get into the open position take the backward position of any scale pattern and move it down the fretboard until your first finger is behind the nut. Any note you would have played with the first finger is now an open string. Check out the following diagrams.

If we go from A natural minor/Aeolian to G natural minor, we shift the whole pattern down 2 frets. The notes on the second fret will become open strings and the key will change to G natural minor.

A Natural Minor Backward Position

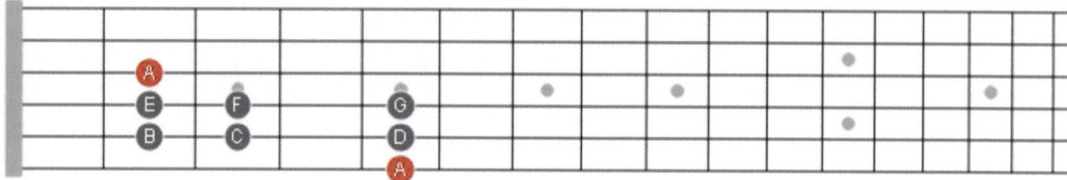

G Natural Minor Open Position

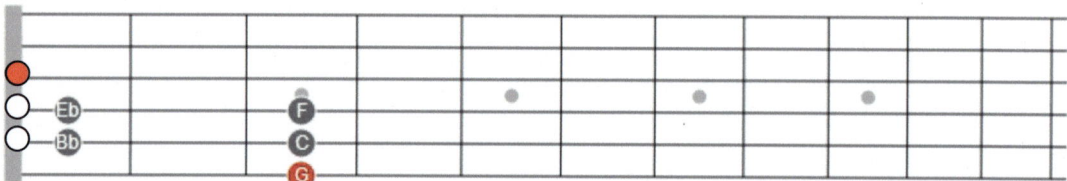

The notes on the second fret become open strings after shifting the pattern two frets closer to the nut.

C Natural Minor Open Position

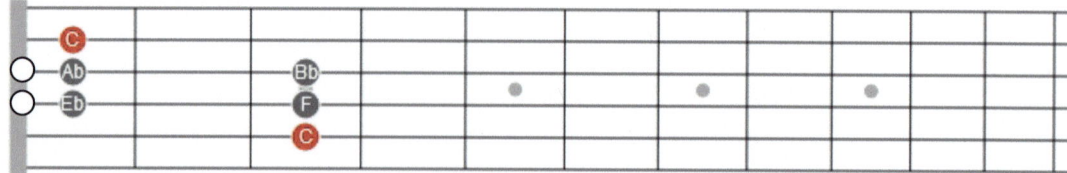

Again, when playing in the warp zone you'll need to make the mental shift. The C note is on the B string so it must shift up one fret while the open strings D and G form part of the scale.

F Natural Minor Open Position

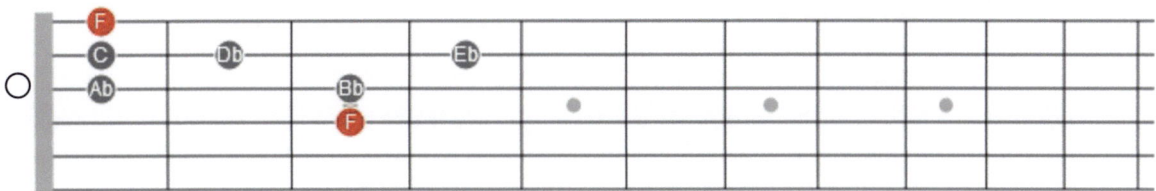

Here both the B and E strings are used so everything is moved up one fret; the only open string that forms part of the scale here is the G string.

Remember: This is the same pattern; the nature of the fretboard warps it. Warping open positions will require a little more time to 'think it out' but this will soon become a natural process.

Arpeggios and the 2 Position System

If you liked the way the 2 Position System simplified scales, then you'll be glad to know that the exact same premise works for arpeggios too! I always found arpeggios incredible tedious to learn, but with the 2 Position System they suddenly became a whole lot more usable. Let's check it out. Remember, an arpeggio is simply the notes of a chord played as single notes.

3-Note Arpeggios

Look at the following 3-note A Minor arpeggio; we'll use the forward and backward positions concept again as we can apply the same method. Just like a minor chord, a minor arpeggio contains the intervals 1, b3, 5 which in A are the notes A, C, E.

Here's the **forward position**:

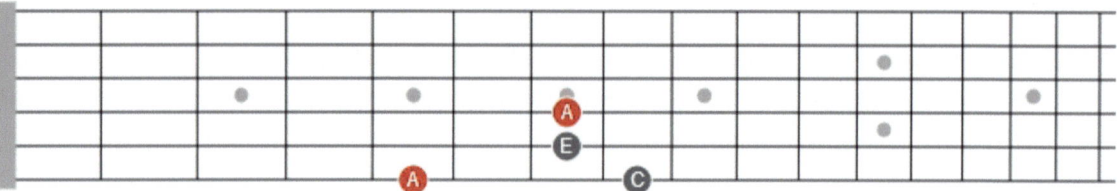

Again, the exact same concepts apply here as they did when we looked at scales. When we move this pattern around the fretboard and invoke the warp factor, the fretboard modifies what is essentially the same pattern.

Here's the forward position on the A, D and G strings. We're not using the B string so it's the same.

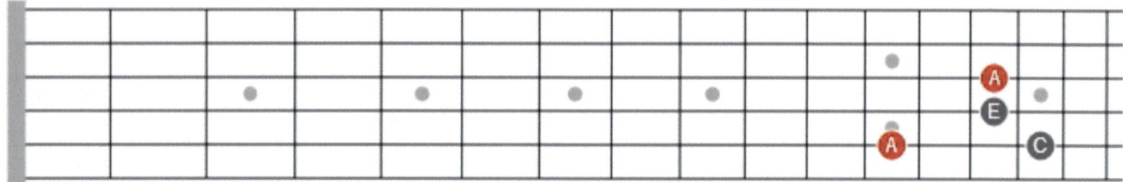

But when we move it across to the next string set (D, G and B), we invoke the warp factor and the A note on the B string must move up one fret but it's still the same pattern. Remember to make this shift in your head as you did with the scale patterns.

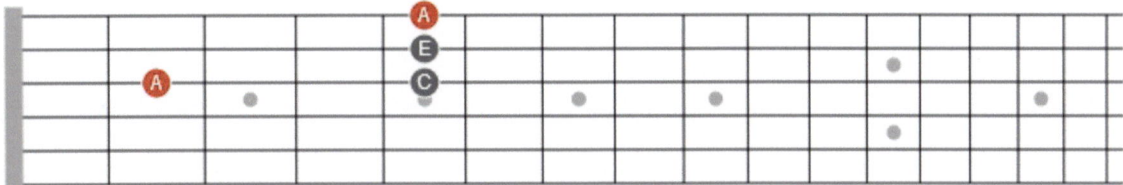

If we then start the pattern on the A on the G string, we're right next to the warp zone so the note(s) on the B string shift up one fret with the top E string following suit. Check it out.

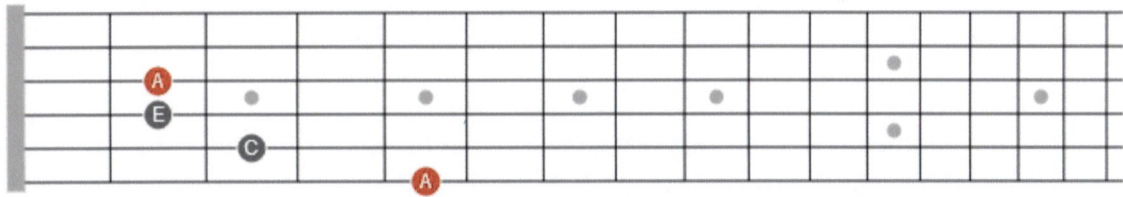

Remember, this is the exact same forward pattern, all that has happened is the notes on the B and E strings have shifted up one fret.

Here's the **backward position**:

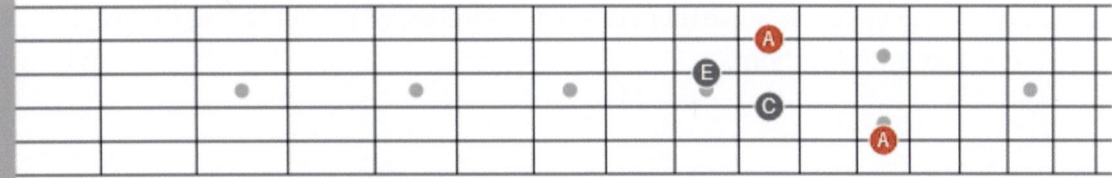

As this position spans four different strings, when we move it across a string set, the warp zone is invoked.

Let's start it on the D string and see what happens.

![fretboard diagram]

Look familiar? Remember this is the backward position with the notes on the top two strings shifted up one fret, and an A Minor chord.

If you want to start this position on the G string, then by all means do so.

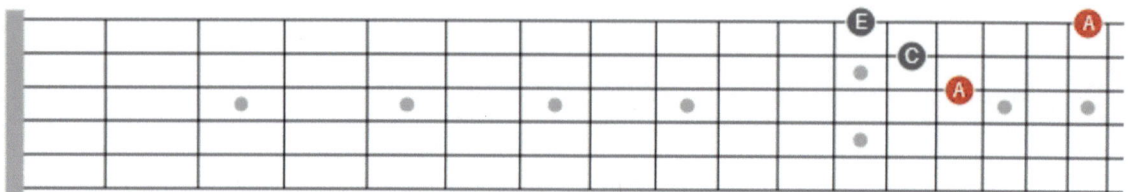

Believe it or not this is still the same original forward pattern (make sure you compare these shapes to the 'unwarped' ones) because the C on the B string shifts up one fret with the E following suit but we 'run out of space', hence the A note at the 17th fret.

Practice moving the forward and backward positions around the fretboard as we did with scales, remembering to take it slowly at first to make sure you know exactly where you are in the arpeggio, and where you're going.

Major Arpeggios

Based on what we just did with the minor arpeggio, your task is to do the same with the major arpeggio. A major arpeggio contains the intervals 1, 3, 5 which in A correspond to the notes A, C#, E. I'll give you the forward and backward positions, then it's up to you to move them around the fretboard remembering to take the warp factor into account.

Major Arpeggio **forward position**:

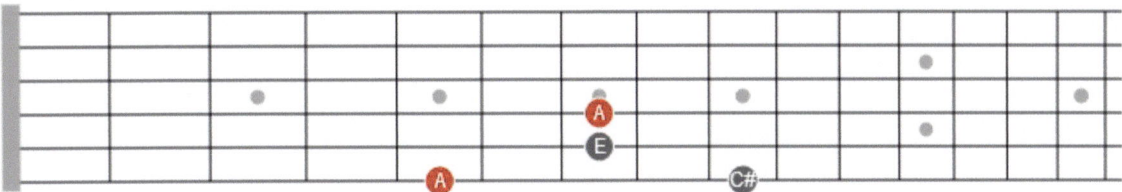

Major Arpeggio **backward position**:

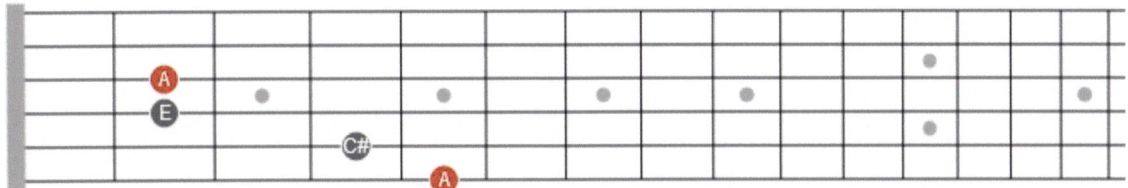

Move the patterns across the fretboard doing the warp shifts in your head. If you hit a wrong note, your ear will tell you as it's much more obvious with arpeggios.

Since we're dealing with 3-note or triad arpeggios here, let's look at the other two basic 3-note triads: the diminished and the augmented triads. Again, I'm only going to give you the forward and backward positions for these arpeggios, so that you can make those mental shifts yourself.

Diminished Arpeggios

A diminished arpeggio contains the intervals 1, b3, b5 which in A correspond to the notes A, C, Eb. Here's the **forward position**:

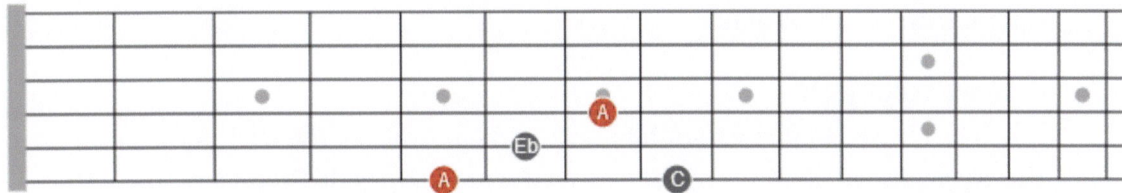

And the **backward position**:

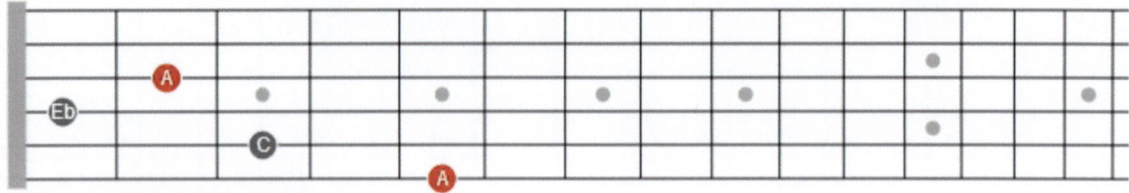

Augmented Arpeggios

An augmented arpeggio contains the intervals 1, 3, #5 which in A are the notes A, C#, E#(F). Here's the **forward position**:

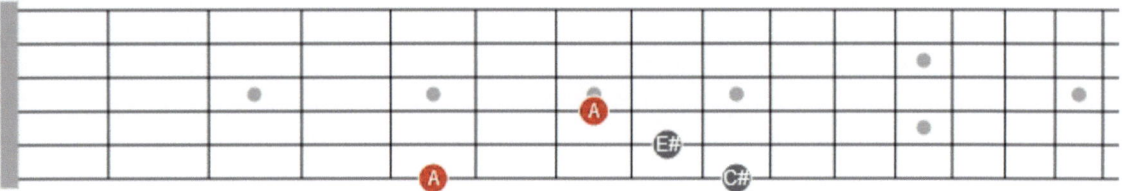

And the **backward position**:

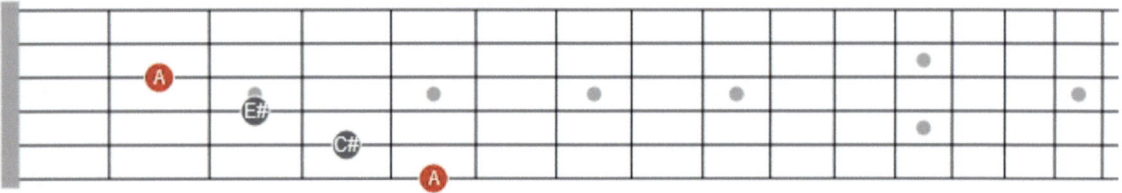

As you start to move the Augmented Arpeggio around the neck, you'll notice that it's symmetrical and a lot of fun.

4-Note Arpeggios

You'll be pleased to know that the previous 8 patterns are the basis for about 95% of the arpeggios you'll ever come across, so the more arpeggios you learn, the faster you'll become at learning them.

Let's look at the most common 4-Note Arpeggios: the major 7, minor 7, dominant 7, minor 7b5, and the minor major 7. As you go through these arpeggios, notice that you're only adding one note to the major, minor and diminished 3-Note ones.

Major 7 Arpeggio (1, 3, 5, 7)
Here are the forward and backward positions for a Major 7 arpeggio:

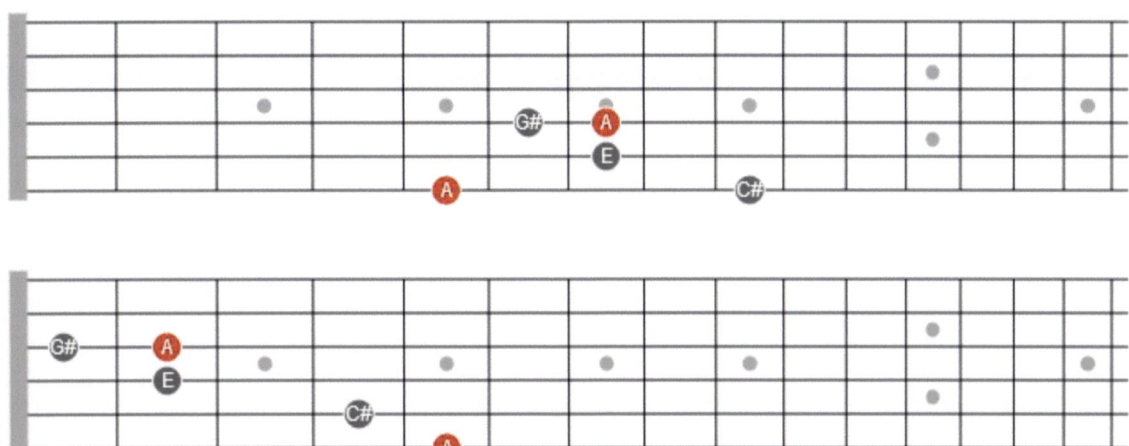

When you start to warp these patterns take it slow so as to avoid rushing and making mistakes.

Minor 7 Arpeggio (1, b3, 5, b7)
Here are the forward and backward positions for a Minor 7 arpeggio:

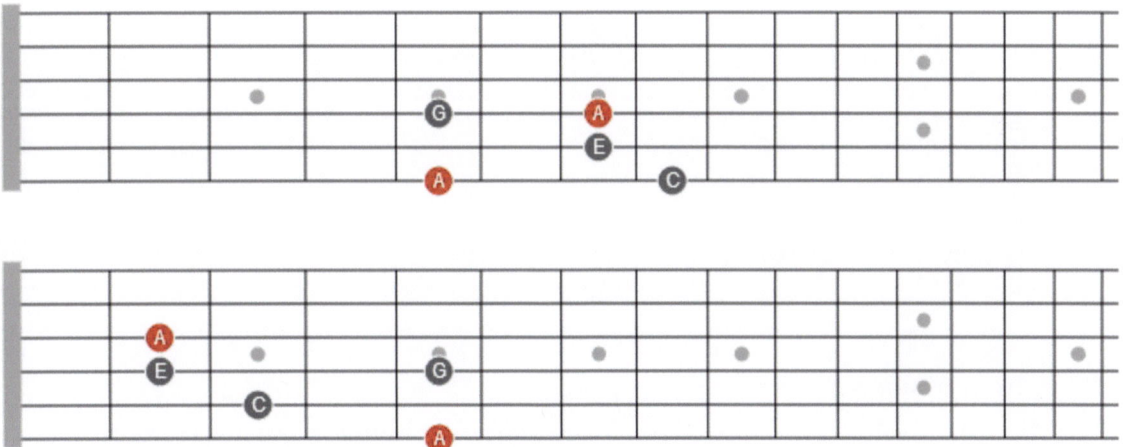

For practical fingering purposes, you'll see that these two patterns also share the G note.

Dominant 7 Arpeggio (1, 3, 5, b7)

Here are the forward and backward positions for a Dominant 7 arpeggio:

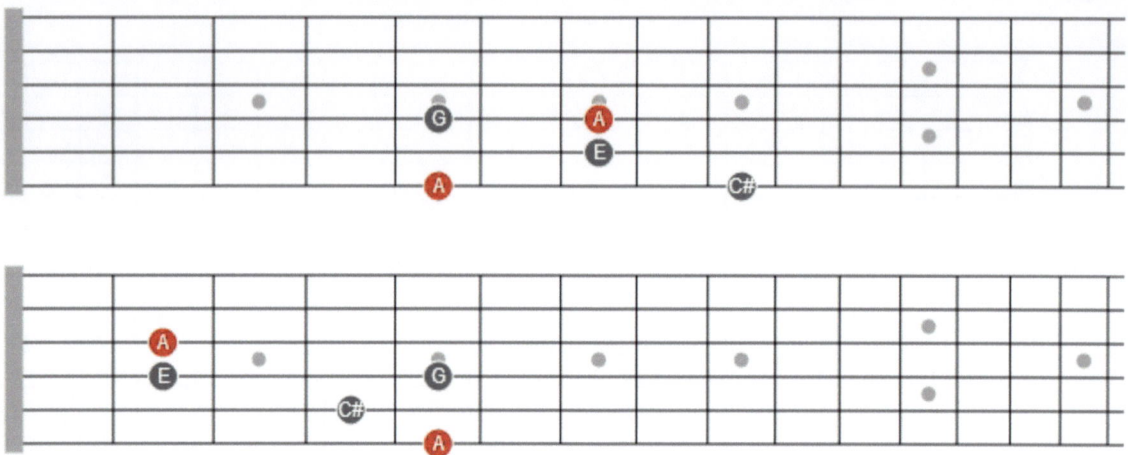

Minor 7b5 Arpeggio (1, b3, b5, b7)

Here are the forward and backward positions for a Diminished 7 arpeggio:

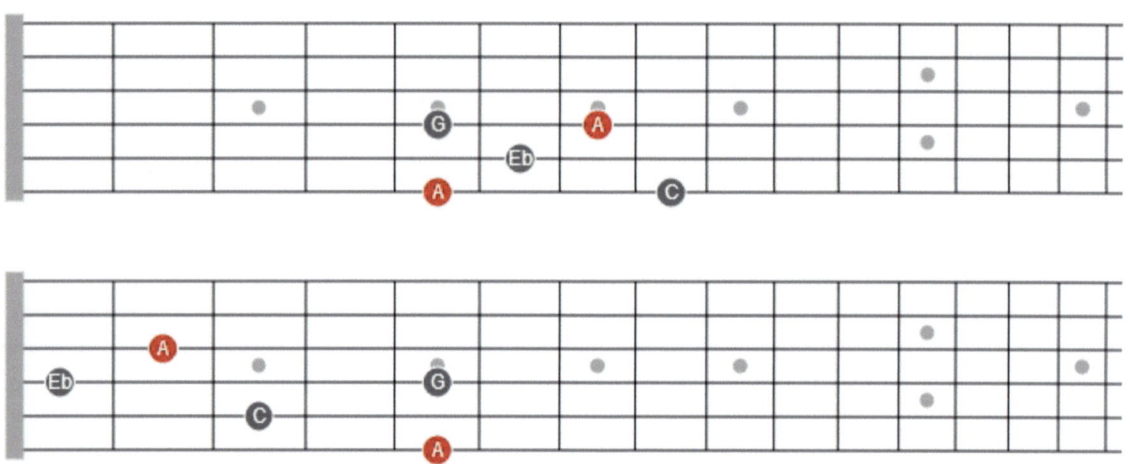

Minor Major 7 Arpeggio (1, b3, 5, 7)

Here are the forward and backward positions for a Minor Major 7 arpeggio:

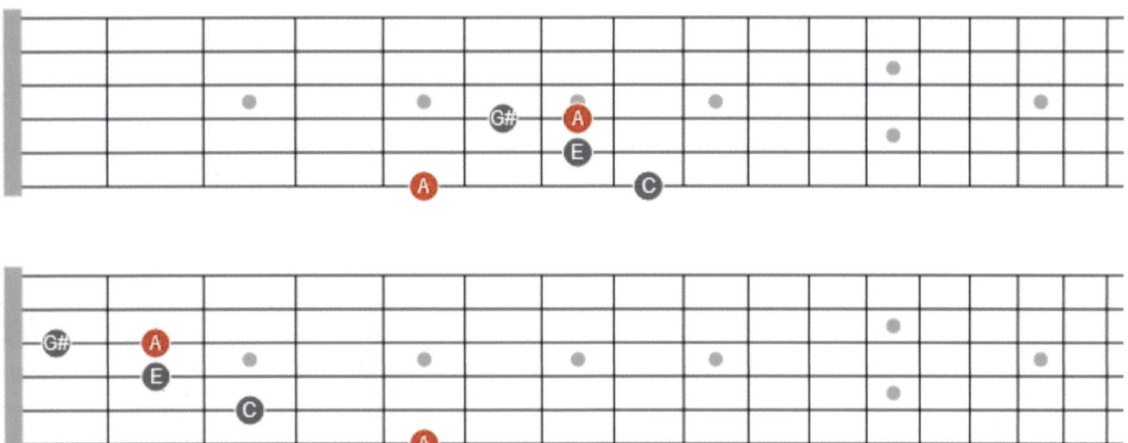

How to Go Beyond 4-Note Arpeggios

The above patterns are by far the most useful ones to know all over the fretboard as regards arpeggios, then if you want to go beyond those patterns you simply add in the upper extensions. We used four of the notes from a seven-note scale to make the above arpeggios, which means there are three notes left over. These are the upper extensions. We've been using A as our starting note, so let's see how this looks using the A Natural Minor Scale:

A	B	C	D	E	F	G	A	B	C	D	E	F	G
1	2	b3	4	5	b6	b7		9		11		b13	

The upper extensions continue the number sequence and these extensions give you arpeggios such as A Minor 9, A Minor 11 etc.

The 2 Position System Applied to Extended Arpeggios

To create 2 Position Patterns for extended arpeggios simply add the upper extension as follows. Here we add the 9(2) to the Minor 7 Arpeggio you already know.

Here are the forward and backward positions for a **Minor 9 Arpeggio (1, b3, 5, b7, 9)**:

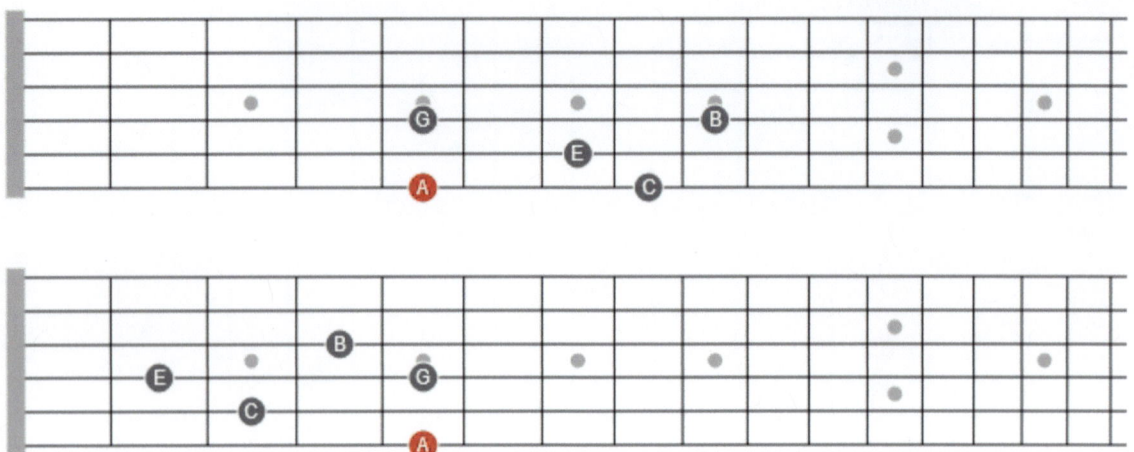

Here are the forward and backward positions for a **Minor 11 Arpeggio (1, b3, 5, b7, 9, 11)**, which is a Minor 7 Arpeggio with an added 9(2) and 11(4).

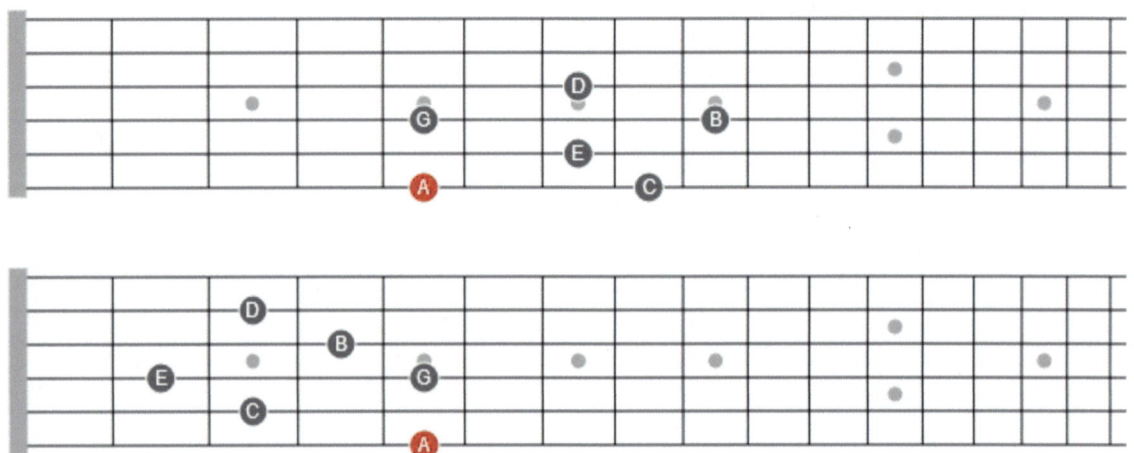

Can you work out the 2 patterns for the Minor 13 arpeggio?

Major 7 Arpeggio Extensions

If we keep adding intervals to the Major 7 Arpeggio, the following happens:

A	B	C#	D	E	F#	G#	A	B	C#	D	E	F#	G#
1	2	3	4	5	6	7		9		11		13	

Here are the forward and backward patterns for the **Major 9 Arpeggio**:

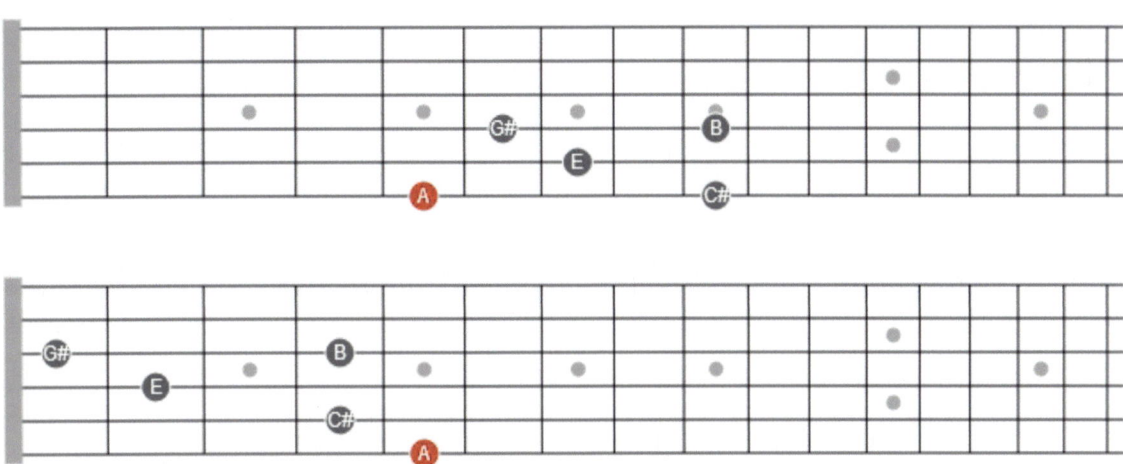

And the **Major 11 Arpeggio**:

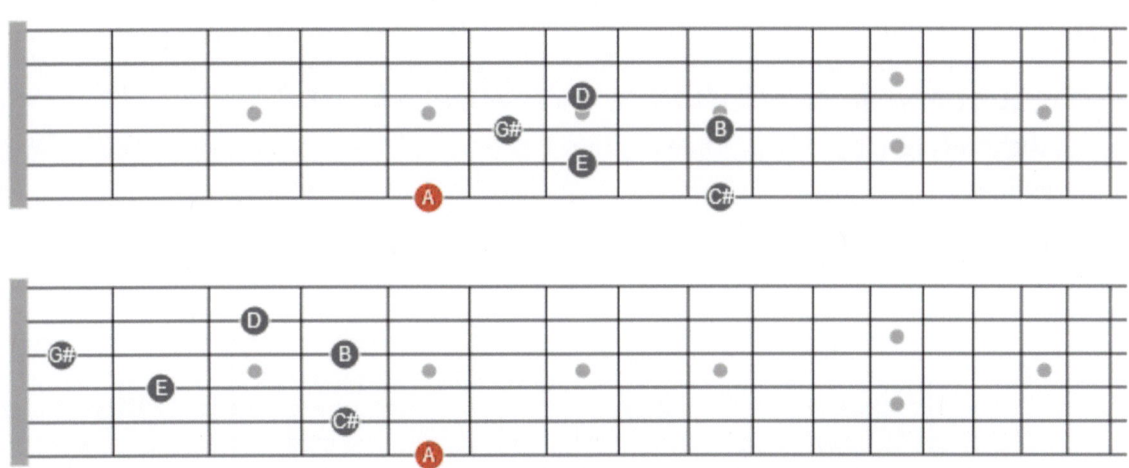

Your fingering for the backward pattern in both these arpeggios should be 4-3-2-1 for the first four notes.

Can you work out the 2 patterns for the Major 13 Arpeggio?

General Rules for Arpeggio Construction

By now you should have a fairly good insight into how arpeggios are constructed in the 2 Position System. You can use the actual notes or the interval pattern to construct them, bearing in mind the following rules:

1. The root note should always be shared between the forward and backward patterns; any other notes that are shared should only be for practical purposes, or due to them falling on open strings.

2. Don't be tempted to ever draw out more than 2 patterns per scale or arpeggio as the warping concept takes care of all the permutations, and all warping must be done mentally for this system to effective.

3. Bear in mind that you will run out of space, or rather the larger patterns won't complete themselves. This is not a problem as long as you know where you are in the arpeggio at all times, and practice moving around the fretboard. Remember that arpeggios, used well, add color to your solos, and this won't happen if you're just playing them up and down in a non-musical, etude style.

4. If you're not sure which notes belong in an arpeggio, break it down into intervals, which will be the same as the chord. For example, a Minor 6 Arpeggio would contain the intervals 1, b3, 5, 6, just like a Minor 6 chord, and the two positions would be as follows:

Forward Position

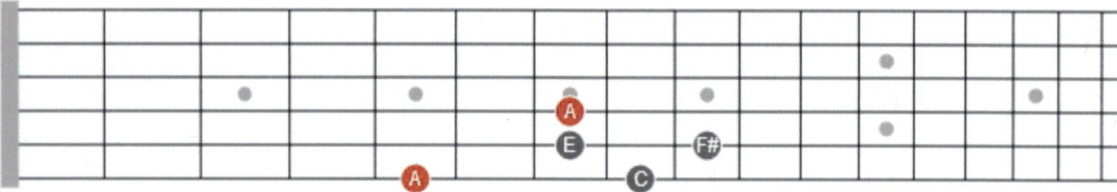

Backward Position

Useful Scales Section

These are the scales I find most useful in most playing situations but feel free to apply the 2 Position System to **any** scale.

I have purposely left out the warped patterns as these must be learned as mental exercises **not** more patterns. I've included some of the more useful modes. This system sees modes as scales in their own right rather than relating them back to the parent major scale. I have found that treating modes as individual scales leads to a far more productive use of them.

Note: m=minor, M=major

Minor Scales

Minor pentatonic forward pattern: (Am, Am7, Asus4, A7sus4)

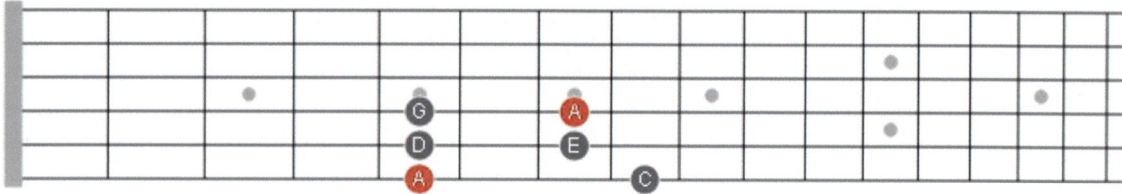

Minor pentatonic backward pattern:

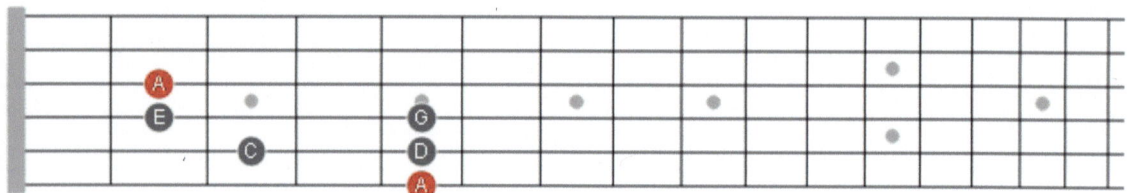

Dorian forward pattern: (Am, Am7, Asus4, Asus2, Am9, Am13, Am6, Amadd9, Am6add9)

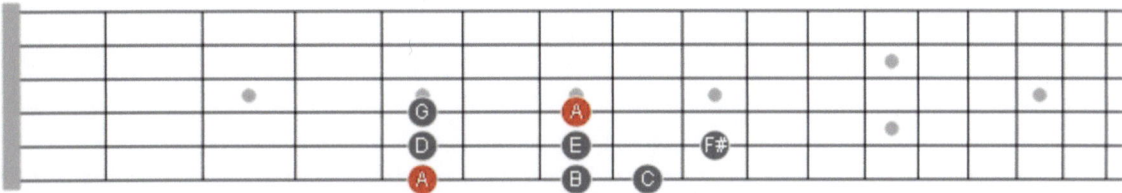

Dorian backward pattern:

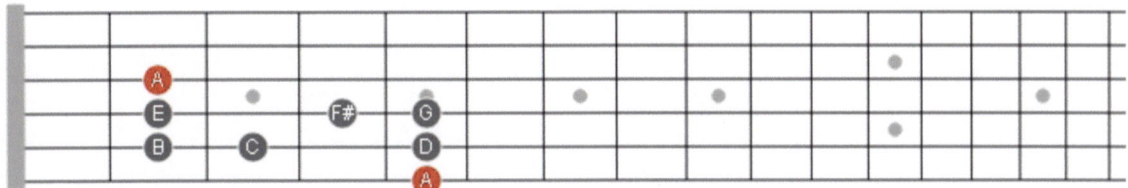

Phrygian forward pattern: (Am, Am7, Asus4, Am7#5, A7sus4)

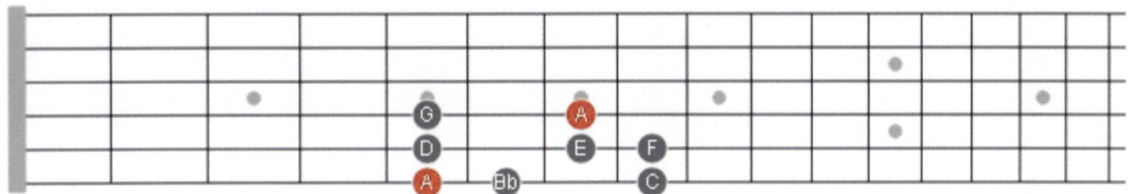

Phrygian backward pattern:

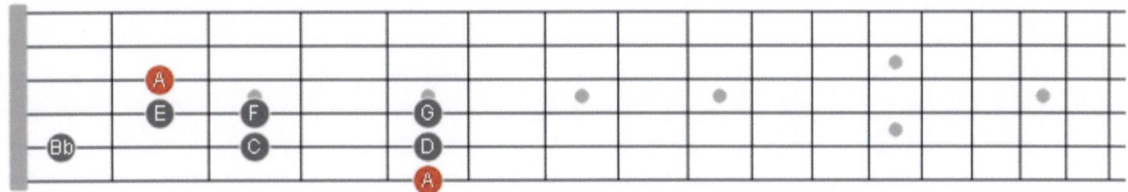

Melodic Minor forward pattern: (Am, AmM7, Am6, Amadd9, Am6add9, AmM9)

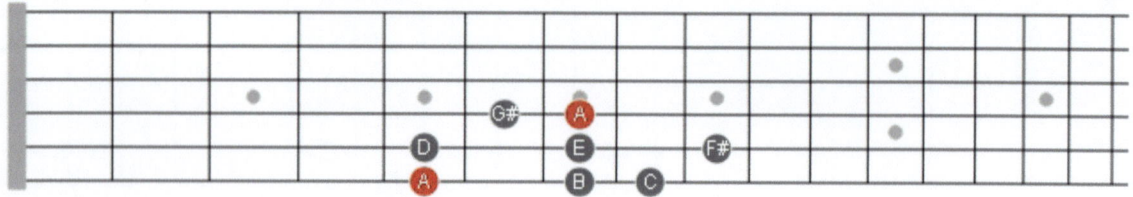

Melodic Minor backward pattern:

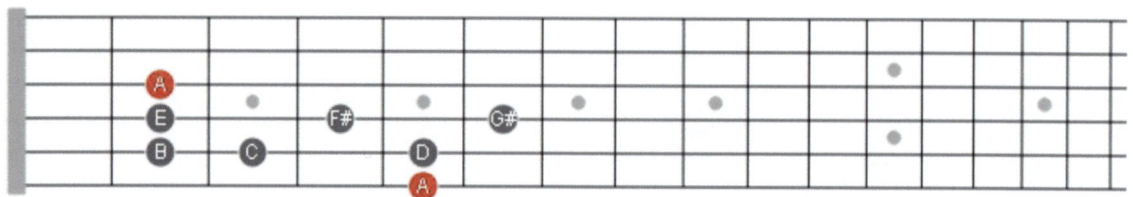

Harmonic Minor forward pattern: (Am, Asus4, Asus2, Amadd9, AmM7, AmM9)

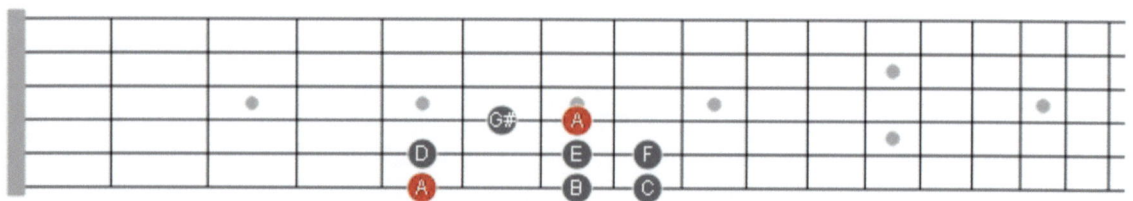

Harmonic Minor backward pattern:

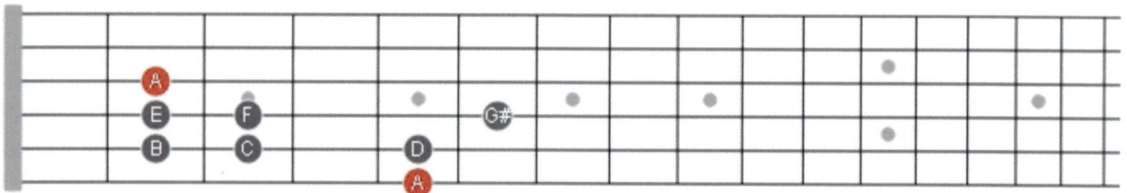

Major Scales

The Major Pentatonic forward position: (A, AM7, Asus2)

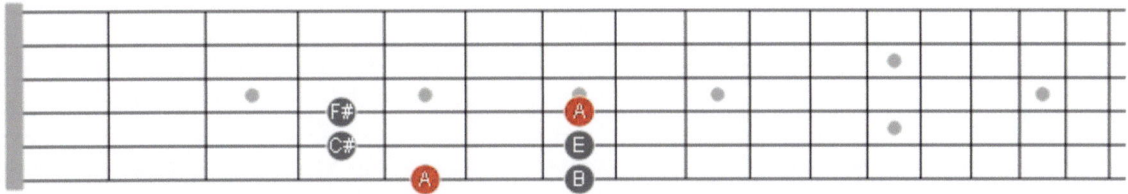

The Major Pentatonic backward position:

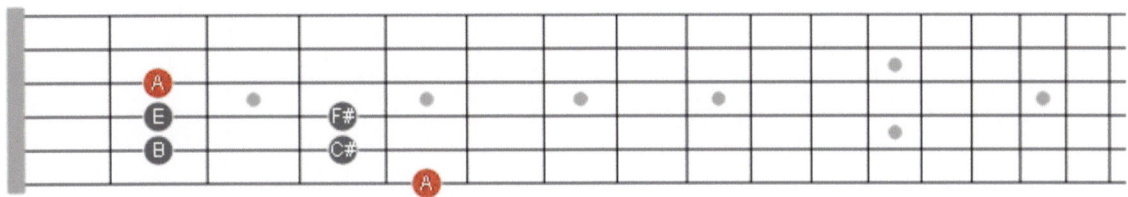

The Major Scale forward pattern: (A, AM7, Aadd9, Asus4, Asus2, AM9, AM13, A6, A6add9)

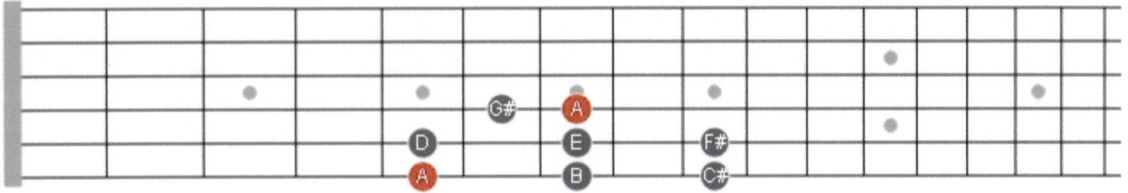

The Major Scale backward pattern:

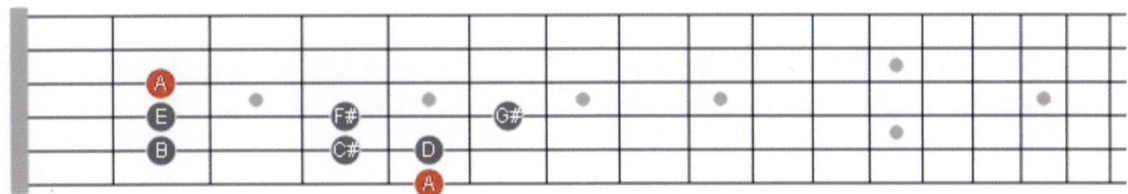

Lydian forward pattern: (A, AM7, Aadd9, Asus2, AM9, AM13, AM9#11, AM13#11, A6, A6add9, AM7b5)

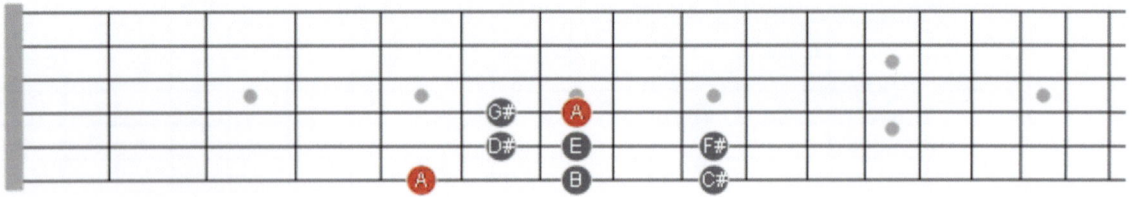

Lydian backward pattern:

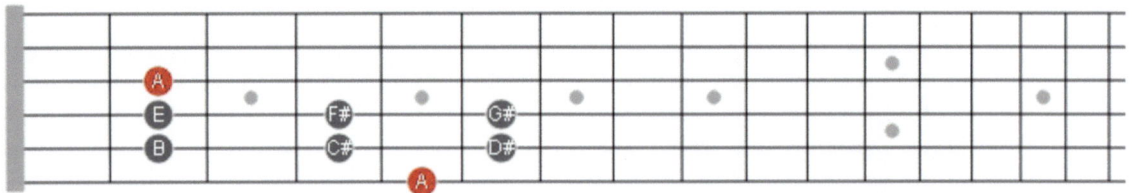

Mixolydian forward pattern: (A, A7, Aadd9, Asus4, Asus2, A6, A6add9, A9, A11, A13, A7sus4)

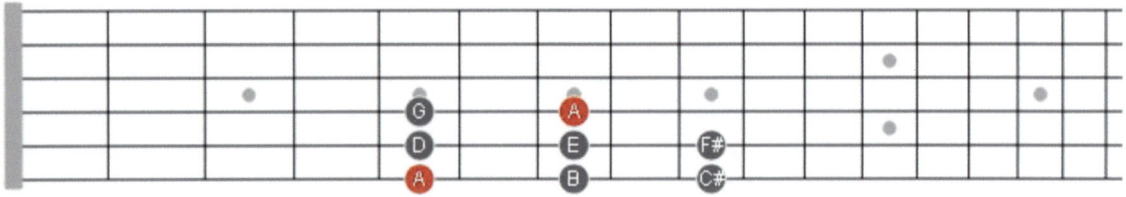

Mixolydian backward pattern:

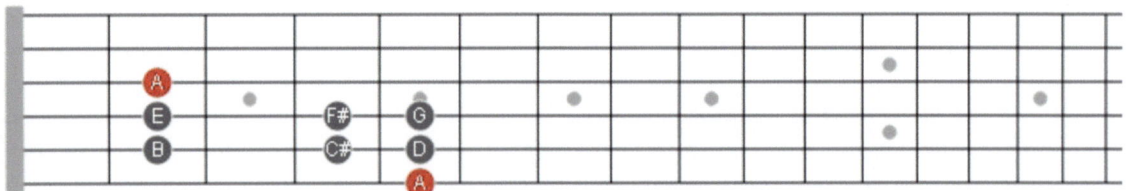

Dominant 7 Scales

Lydian b7 forward pattern: (A, A7, Aadd9, Asus2, A6, A6add9, A9, A13, A7b5, A9b5, A13#11)

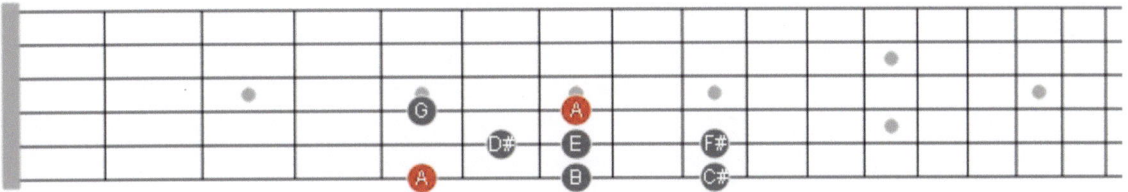

Lydian b7 backward pattern:

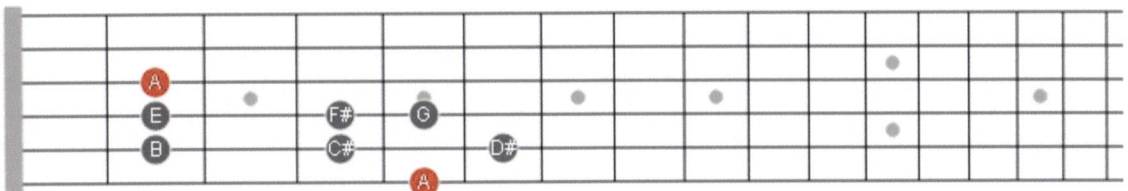

Mixolydian b6 forward pattern: (A, A7, Aadd9, A+, Asus4, Asus2, A9, A11, A7sus4, A7#5, A9#5)

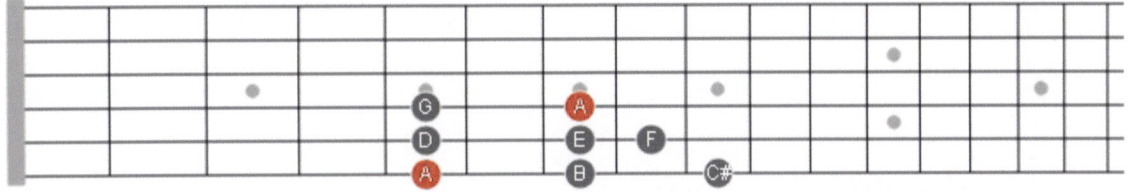

Mixolydian b6 backward pattern:

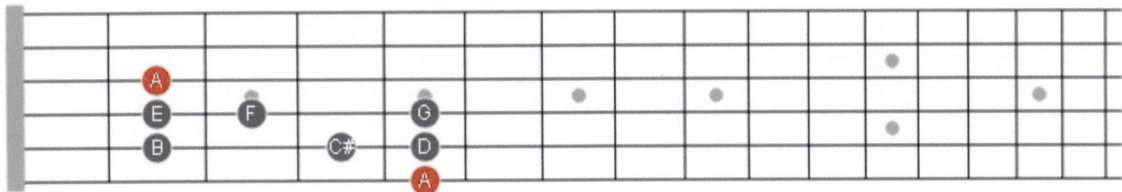

The Blues Scale forward pattern: (Am, Am7, Adim, Asus4, Am7b5, A7sus4)

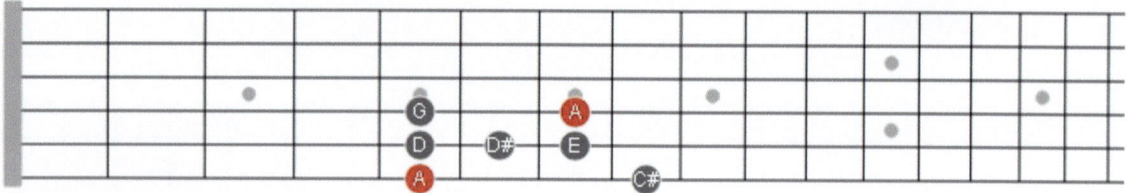

The Blues Scale backward pattern:

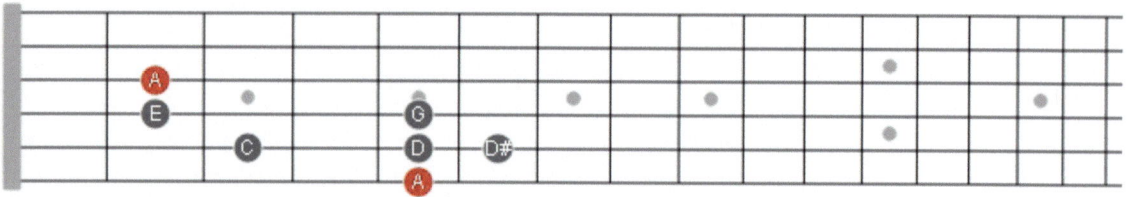

Other Useful Scales
Whole tone forward pattern: (A+, A7b5, A7#5, A9b5, A9#5)

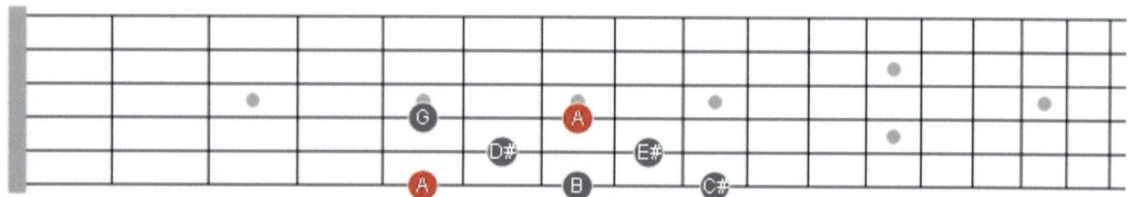

Whole tone backward pattern:

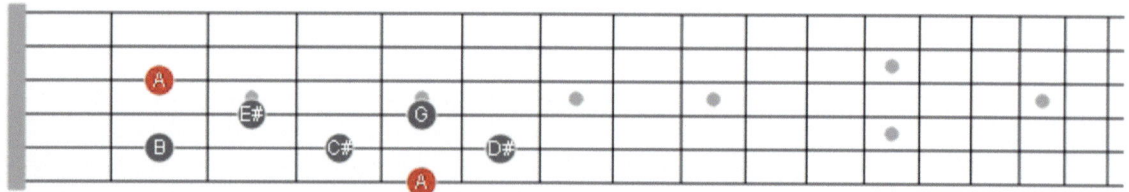

Diminshed scale forward pattern: (Adim, Adim7)

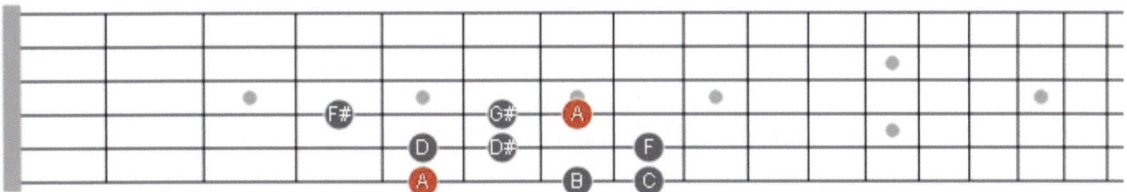

Diminshed scale backward pattern:

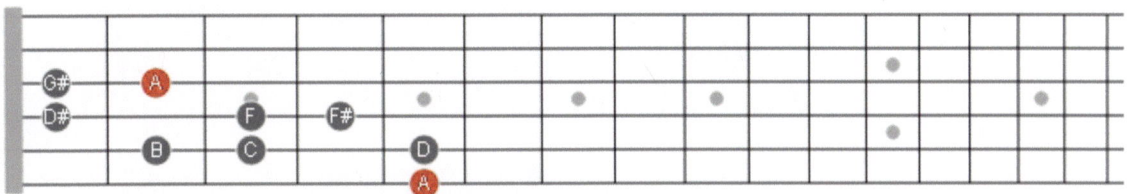

Locrian forward pattern: (Adim, Am7b5, Am7#5)

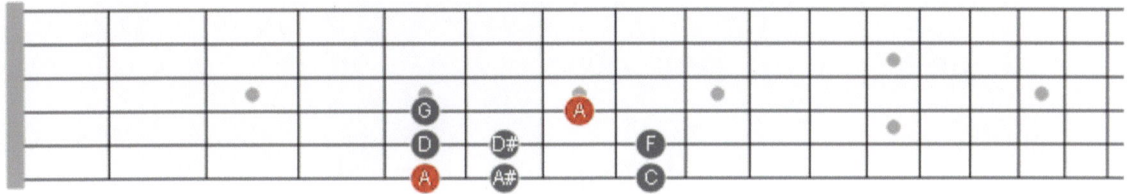

Locrian backward pattern:

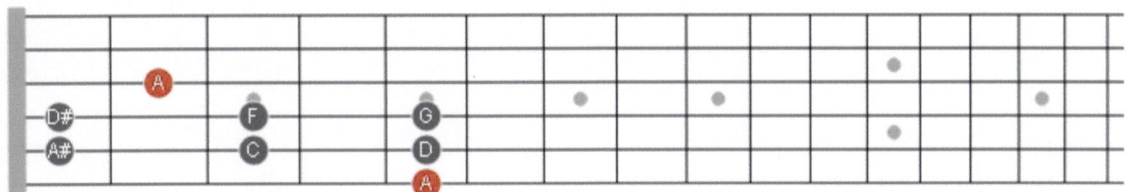

More from Unlock the Guitar

Visit www.unlocktheguitar.net for more insight into all things guitar on the **blog**, and our extensive selection of eBooks on scales, chords, and the bestselling guitar hacks series.

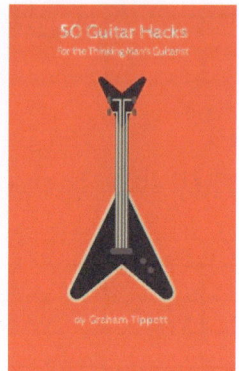
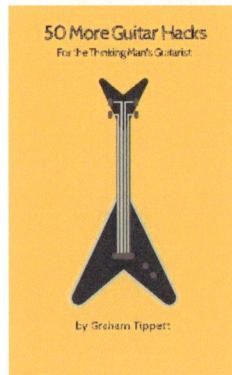
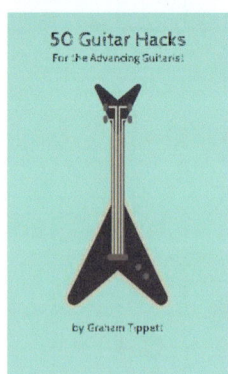

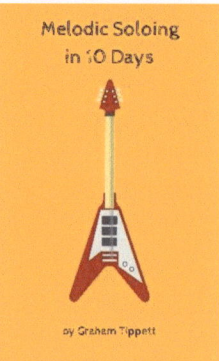

Printed in France by Amazon
Brétigny-sur-Orge, FR